Aberdeenshire Library and Information Service
www.aberdeenshire.gov.uk.libraries
Renewals Hotline 01224 661511

Make and Eat

Sandwiches & Snacks

Susannah Blake

WAYLAND

First published in 2008
by Wayland

Copyright © Wayland 2008

Wayland
338 Euston Road
London NW1 3BH

Wayland
Level 17/207 Kent Street
Sydney NSW 2000

Senior editor: Jennifer Schofield
Designer: Jane Hawkins
Photographer: Andy Crawford
Proofreader: Susie Brooks

The author and publisher would like to thank the following
models: Adam Menditta, Jade Campbell, Demi Mensah, Robert
Kilminster, Taylor Fulton, Kaine Zachary Levy, Ammar Duffus.

Blake, Susannah
  Sandwiches & snacks. - (Make & eat)
  1. Snack foods - Juvenile literature 2. Sandwiches -
  Juvenile literature 3. Cookery - Juvenile literature
  I. Title
  641.5'3

ISBN: 978 0 7502 5354 3

Printed in China

Wayland is a division of Hachette Children's Books,
an Hachette Livre UK company.

Note to parents and teachers:

The recipes in this book are designed
to be made by children. However, we
recommend adult supervision at all times
as the Publisher cannot be held
responsible for any injury caused while
making these recipes.

Contents

All about sandwiches and snacks

Most sandwiches are made from two slices of bread with a filling spread in between. You can make all kinds of different sandwich depending on your choice of bread and filling. Snacks are usually smaller than a meal and can be anything from a crunchy apple to potato wedges and a dip. Snacks should be easy to make and just enough to fill a gap.

MAKING A SANDWICH

Choosing the bread for your sandwich is important because the type of bread you choose, will give the sandwich a particular taste and texture. Bread can be white, brown or wholemeal, or it can be made of rye, corn or other grains. Shaped breads, such as a French baguette or a bread roll, are good for turning into chunky sandwiches. Pitta breads can be split and the filling stuffed inside, while flatbreads, such as tortillas, can be rolled up around the filling to make a wrap.

You can put all kinds of filling inside your sandwich. They can be sweet or savoury and you can add just one filling or you might decide to have several. Popular fillings include jam, cheese, ham, egg, tuna, chicken and hummus. You can also add salad, such as sliced cucumber and tomato, cress, lettuce and coleslaw. You might also want to add extra flavourings such as pickle, chutney or mayonnaise.

SIMPLE SNACKS

Different types of snack are eaten all over the world. For example, if you lived in Italy, you may have some homemade bruschetta – tomato toasts – with some olives as an afternoon snack. If you lived in Mexico, nachos or quesadillas would be perfect to keep you going. Just like sandwiches, snacks can be sweet or savoury. Although snacks such as crisps, cakes and biscuits are delicious, they are not very healthy and should be eaten only as a treat. Instead, snack on fruit and vegetables, such as oranges, bananas and carrots.

GET STARTED!

In this book you can learn to make a whole range of sandwiches and snacks. All the recipes use everyday kitchen equipment, such as knives, spoons, forks and chopping boards. You can see pictures of some of the different equipment that you may need on page 23. Before you start, check that you have all the equipment that you will need and make a list of any ingredients that you need to buy. Make sure there is an adult to help you, especially with the recipes that involve using the cooker or oven.

When you have everything you need, make sure all the kitchen surfaces are clean and wash your hands well with soap and water. If you have long hair, tie it back. Always wash raw fruit and vegetables under cold running water before preparing or cooking them. This will help to remove any dirt and germs. Then, put on an apron and get cooking!

Creamy raita

This Indian dip is great for scooping up with poppadums. If you do not have poppadums, you could serve it with strips of red and orange peppers.

INGREDIENTS

For 4 servings:
- 1/2 large cucumber
- 225ml Greek yogurt
- 1 garlic clove, peeled
- 2 tbsp fresh mint
- pinch of salt
- poppadums to serve

EXTRA EQUIPMENT
- sieve

1 Cut the cucumber in half lengthways. Using a teaspoon, scrape out the seeds from each half and throw them away.

2 Grate each cucumber half. Be careful not to rub your fingers on the grater.

3 Put the cucumber in a sieve and hold it over the kitchen sink. Press down on the cucumber with your hand to squeeze out as much liquid as possible.

4 Tip the cucumber into a medium-sized bowl and add the yogurt.

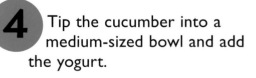

5 Crush the garlic in a garlic press and add it to the cucumber and yogurt.

6 To chop the mint, pluck off the leaves from the stems until you have a small handful of leaves. Roll the leaves into a loose ball and gently rock a knife over the leaves. Do this until the leaves are finely chopped.

7 Add the mint and a pinch of salt to the yogurt and stir well. Taste the mixture and, if necessary, add a pinch more salt and stir.

8 Put the minty yogurt into a serving bowl and serve with the poppadums.

MINTY CURES

Mint not only adds flavour to food but it also has healing properties. Next time you have a tummy ache, put some mint leaves in hot water. Leave the water to cool, then sip the minty tea.

Hummus wrap

A wrap is a kind of sandwich, but instead of putting the filling between two slices of bread, you roll it up inside a single flatbread. You can put all kinds of sandwich filling inside a wrap. When you have mastered this one, why not try another filling?

INGREDIENTS

For 1 serving:
- 1/4 red pepper
- 1 tortilla wrap
- 2 tbsp hummus
- handful of salad leaves

1 Put the pepper on the chopping board and gently pull out any seeds and left-over pith. Cut the pepper into small pieces and set them aside for later.

2 Put the tortilla on a board and spread the hummus over it.

DELICIOUS HUMMUS

To make your own hummus, rinse and drain a tin of chickpeas. Blend them together with 1 crushed clove of garlic, 1 teaspoon of ground cumin, 1 teaspoon of ground coriander, 4 tablespoons of olive oil, 2 tablespoons of lemon juice and 1 tablespoon of tahini (sesame seed paste).

3 Sprinkle the chopped pepper over one half of the tortilla.

4 Scatter the salad leaves on top of the chopped pepper.

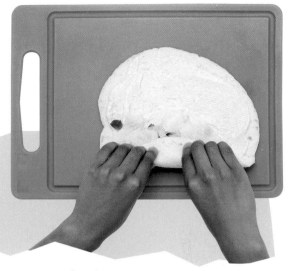

5 To roll up the tortilla, start rolling from the edge of the half that has the salad and peppers. Tuck in any stray leaves as you roll. The half of the wrap that is covered with hummus but has no chopped pepper or salad leaves will help to stick the wrap together.

6 Cut the wrap in half across the middle to make two smaller wraps. Put them on a plate and serve.

9

Classic egg mayo

If you like this classic recipe, try putting a few slices of cucumber or tomato on top of the egg mixture or adding a sprinkling of cress. You could try using different types of bread, such as rye or a baguette, too.

INGREDIENTS

For 1 serving:
- 1 egg • water
- 1 tbsp mayonnaise
- 2 slices wholegrain bread
- salt and black pepper

Ask an adult to help you use the cooker.

1 Put the egg in a small saucepan and pour cold water over the top to cover the egg by about 3cm.

2 Bring the water to the boil – when you see bubbles, the water is boiling. Turn down the heat and let the water simmer gently for 10 minutes.

FRESH EGGS

As an egg gets older, the white and yolk start to change. If you compared a very fresh egg with a ten-day old egg and a 20-day old egg you would see a big difference. The very fresh egg would have a fat, rounded yolk and two layers of white. As an egg gets older, the yolk becomes flatter and the difference between the two layers of white becomes less and less until you can hardly notice it at all.

3 Turn off the heat and take the egg out of the water using a slotted spoon. Put the egg in a bowl of cold water and leave it to cool.

4 When the egg is cool, tap it against your work surface until the shell is cracked all over. Peel off the shell and rinse the egg under cold water to remove any left-over bits of shell.

5 Cut the egg into small pieces and put it in a clean bowl.

6 Add the mayonnaise, a pinch of salt and a grinding of black pepper to the egg and stir to mix.

7 Put a slice of bread on the board and spread the egg mixture on top of it.

8 Place the second slice of bread on top and press down gently to make sure it is secure. Cut your sandwich in half from corner to corner to serve.

Bruschetta

Open sandwiches are ones that do not have a second slice of bread on top. Bruschetta are little Italian toasts that come somewhere between a mini open sandwich and a snack.

INGREDIENTS

For 4 servings:
- 2 tomatoes
- 1 1/4 tsp olive oil
- 1 small baguette
- 1 garlic clove
- 8 fresh basil leaves
- salt and black pepper

Ask an adult to help you use the grill.

1 Cut each tomato in half. Using your thumb, gently press out the seeds and jelly and throw them away.

2 Finely chop the tomatoes and put them in a bowl. Sprinkle a pinch of salt and a grinding of black pepper over the tomatoes. Then pour over 1 teaspoon of the olive oil and stir the mixture gently. Set aside for later.

3 Wipe and dry the chopping board. Cut off the end of the baguette, then cut eight slices, about 1.5cm thick.

4 Turn on the grill. If it is an electric grill, leave it to heat up for about 5 minutes. Arrange the bread slices on the grill rack and toast them so that both sides are golden.

5 Arrange the toasts on a serving plate. Cut the garlic clove in half and rub the cut side over the top of each slice of toast. Garlic has a very strong taste, so you only need to rub the toasts gently to give them a good garlicky flavour.

6 Spoon the chopped tomatoes and any juices from the bowl on top of the toasts. Drizzle the rest of the olive oil over each of the toasts.

7 Top each of the toasts with a basil leaf before you serve the bruschetta.

ANTIPASTI

In Italy, little snacks such as bruschetta, olives, marinated vegetables and cold meats are served as an appetizer before the main meal. These little snacks are called antipasti, which means 'before the meal'.

Quesadilla wedges

Quesadillas are a kind of fried sandwich from Mexico. This quesadilla is made with plain cheese, but in Mexico chillies, vegetables, such as spinach or peppers, and ham are used in quesadillas.

INGREDIENTS

For 4 servings:
- 60g Cheddar cheese
- 2 plain tortillas
- ground black pepper

Ask an adult to help you use the cooker.

1 Grate the cheese onto a small plate. Be careful not to grate your fingers!

2 Heat a large non-stick frying pan over a medium heat.

GRATE AWAY

The easiest way to grate cheese is to use a box-shaped cheese grater. Hold the grater firmly in one hand on a plate or board. Hold the block of cheese in the other hand and hold it against the top of the grater. Slide the cheese down against the teeth of the grater and shreds of cheese will fall down inside the grater. Continue in the same way until you have grated enough cheese for your recipe.

3 Put a tortilla in the pan. Sprinkle the cheese over the tortilla in an even layer and grind over some black pepper.

4 Put the second tortilla on top of the cheese and cook for about 3 minutes until the bottom tortilla is crisp and golden underneath. Check by lifting up the edge of the tortilla with a spatula.

5 Slide the spatula under the tortilla and carefully flip over the whole quesadilla.

6 Cook for a further 2 minutes until the quesadilla is golden on the second side.

7 Carefully slide the quesadilla onto a large chopping board and cut it in half. Cut it in half again so that you have four quarters. Then cut each quarter in half to make 8 wedges.

8 Pile the quesadilla wedges onto a plate and serve them straight away, on their own or with some tomato salsa for dipping.

Chunky wedges and dip

These potato wedges make a really filling snack or a lunchtime treat. Be careful when you eat them as they will be piping hot when you take them out of the oven!

INGREDIENTS

For 4 servings:
- 1 large potato, scrubbed and patted dry
- 1 tbsp olive oil
- salt and ground black pepper
- 100ml natural yogurt
- 2 tsp pesto

Ask an adult to help you use the oven.

1 Preheat the oven to 190°C/375°F/Gas 5.

2 Cut the potato in half. Place the two halves on their flat sides and cut them into quarters. Cut each quarter into chunky wedges – like big chips.

POTATOES

Today potatoes are eaten all over the world. However, this was not always the case. The very first potatoes were grown in South America and there is evidence that they were eaten in Peru as far back as 2,000 years ago. Europeans first tasted potatoes in 1537 in what is now Colombia. In the 1550s, potatoes were brought to Spain and then, in 1590, to Britain.

3 Put the potato wedges in a roasting tin in a single layer. Brush on the olive oil, sprinkle over a pinch of salt and grind over some black pepper. Toss to coat the wedges so that they are glossy all over.

4 Bake the wedges for about 20 minutes. Wearing oven gloves, take the tin out of the oven and put it on a heatproof surface. Use a spatula to turn over the wedges. Put the roasting tin back in the oven, and bake the wedges for another 15 minutes until they are golden all over and tender.

5 Meanwhile, stir together the yogurt and pesto and spoon the mixture into a serving bowl.

6 When the potatoes are golden, wearing oven gloves, remove the roasting tin from the oven and lift the wedges onto a serving dish. Serve hot with the dip.

Chicken pitta pocket

You can buy ready-grilled chicken breasts for this recipe – or you can ask an adult to grill a chicken breast for you. You could also use left-over cold roast chicken.

1 Cut off each end of the carrot. Using a vegetable peeler, peel off the skin.

2 Grate the carrot and put the grated pieces in a medium-sized bowl.

3 Put the chicken on the board and cut it into bite-sized pieces. Add it to the grated carrot.

4 To make the dressing, put the sweet chilli sauce, olive oil and vinegar into a small bowl. Add a pinch of salt and stir the mixture well.

5 Pour the dressing over the carrots and chicken and mix it well.

6 Turn on the grill. If you are using an electric grill, leave it for about 5 minutes to heat it up. Put the pitta bread under the grill and warm it for a few minutes on each side until it starts to puff up.

7 Put the bread on the board – it will be full of hot steam that can burn, so be careful! Cut the bread in half and carefully open up the halves to make two pockets.

8 Put a couple of salad leaves in each pitta pocket, then spoon the chicken and carrot salad on top. Eat warm or cold.

PITTA BREAD

This soft, chewy flatbread is eaten all over the Middle East. It is made of wheat and is slightly leavened. When it is baked, the oval-shaped bread puffs up, leaving it hollow inside. This hollow makes a kind of pocket that makes pitta bread perfect for stuffing to make a kind of sandwich.

Tuna melt

This is a classic open sandwich topped with tuna mayonnaise and melting cheese. Adding chopped cornichon or dill pickle to the tuna mixture adds a tangy bite, but if you prefer to leave it out, the tuna also tastes great on its own.

INGREDIENTS

For 2 servings:
- 200g can tuna, drained
- 2 cornichons or 1 large dill pickle (optional)
- 3 tbsp mayonnaise
- freshly ground black pepper
- 2 thick slices bread
- 2 large slices Jarlsberg or Swiss cheese such as Emmental

Ask an adult to help you use the grill.

1 Put the tuna in a bowl and break it up into flakes using a fork.

2 If using cornichons or dill pickle, put them on a board and chop finely. Add them to the tuna.

3 Add the mayonnaise and a grinding of black pepper to the tuna. Mix everything together.

4 Turn on the grill. If you are using an electric grill, leave it for about 5 minutes to heat up. Arrange the bread slices on the grill pan and place them under the grill for a few minutes to toast one side.

5 Spread the untoasted side of bread with the tuna mixture.

6 Top each slice of toast with a slice of cheese and then place the toast under the grill until the cheese bubbles.

7 Carefully slide the toasts onto plates. You could serve the toast with a side salad of coleslaw.

HOLES IN CHEESE

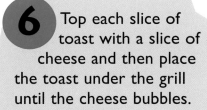

Both Jarlsberg and Emmental cheese are made in similar ways and have the same kind of mild flavour. They are both full of holes, too. The holes appear when the cheese is made. Several bacteria are used to make the cheeses and while the cheeses mature, the bacteria produce carbon dioxide. This gas forms big bubbles in the cheese, which makes the holes.

Glossary

bacteria

Invisibly small organisms that cannot been seen without a microscope. Some bacteria are good for us but many, such as germs, can make us ill.

carbon dioxide

A colourless gas. Carbon dioxide makes bubbles in certain types of cheese and these bubbles make holes in the cheese.

filling

The ingredients that go between the bread in a sandwich. Eggs, tuna and cheese are all popular sandwich fillings.

hollow
Empty.

leavened
When dough has risen it is leavened. Ingredients such as yeast and baking powder are known as leavening ingredients as they cause dough to rise.

marinated
When something is left to soak in a sauce. Oils and vinegars are often used as marinades.

Middle East

The countries to the east of the Mediterranean Sea, from Egypt to Iran.

mild

Not very strong. Jarlsberg cheese has a mild flavour.

poppadums

An Indian flatbread that is thin and crispy. Poppadums are usually eaten with dips or chutneys.

rye

A cereal used to make bread and biscuits. Rye is similar in colour to wholemeal.

savoury

When flavours are tasty but not sweet. For example, cheese has a savoury flavour.

tahini

A savoury dip that is made from sesame seeds. Tahini is usually used in Middle Eastern food.

texture
The way the surface of something feels.

yolk
The yellow of an egg.

EXTRA INFORMATION

These abbreviations have been used:
• tbsp – tablespoon • tsp – teaspoon
• ml – millilitre • g – gram • l – litre

To work out where the cooker dial needs to be for high, medium and low heat, count the marks on the dial and divide it by three. The top few are high and the bottom few are low. The in-between ones are medium.

Equipment

MEASURING SPOONS
Measuring spoons help you to use the exact amount of ingredients.

SLOTTED SPOON
This spoon is useful for taking solid food out of liquids as the liquid drains through the holes.

MEASURING CUPS
These are used just like measuring spoons but for measuring bigger quantities of ingredients.

GARLIC PRESS
Crush garlic finely by putting a peeled garlic clove inside the press and squeezing the handle.

PASTRY BRUSH
Use to brush marinades and oil onto foods.

CHOPPING BOARDS
These protect your work surface. Make sure you keep your chopping boards clean and always use a different one for meat and vegetables.

ROASTING TRAY
Use this metal pan for roasting meat and vegetables in the oven.

KNIVES
Be careful when chopping and always keep your fingers away from the sharp blade.

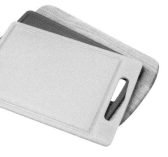

FRYING PAN
Use this pan to fry food. You need to add very little butter or oil to a non-stick pan.

BOX GRATER
Use to grate food such as cheese and carrots. Keep your fingers away from the sharp teeth of the grater.

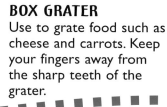

Index